SALTATIONS

SALTATIONS

JENNIFER STILL

thistledown press

Library and Archives Canada Cataloguing in Publication

Still, Jennifer, 1973-
Saltations / Jennifer Still.

Poems.
ISBN 1-894345-96-7

I. Title.

PS8637.T54S24 2005   C811'.6   C2005-905113-2

Cover and book design by Jackie Forrie
Printed in Canada

Thistledown Press Ltd.
633 Main Street, Saskatoon, Saskatchewan, S7H 0J8
www.thistledown.sk.ca

Canada Council   Conseil des Arts
for the Arts   du Canada

SASKATCHEWAN
ARTS BOARD

Canadian   Patrimoine
Heritage   canadien

Thistledown Press gratefully acknowledges the financial assistance of the Canada Council for the Arts, the Saskatchewan Arts Board, and the Government of Canada through the Book Publishing Industry Development Program for its publishing program.

for my grandmothers
in memory of Fanny Davies (Tapper)

A HINGED AIR

It's not so much that you can't see
depth but that everything is within
reach. The sky already teaching you
limits of the hand, cloud already
an interval of believing.

It's not so much the light you teach me, but the waste
of colour, how I have spent so much time
on concealment, the absence of white, a misreading
of cloud. Or that the sky

in the puddle in the middle of the street is a girl
poking up at the soles of your feet, a girl
haloed, wide-eyed, in a second sun, sinking.

And that the flame, the flame from the other side of the yard,
is a candle lapping up the wicks of my legs, a cry, yours,
mummymummy, hot, a tug of wax
melting, tears.

Or how the moth is a bow
flitting yellow from your hair, the steam
off my cup, a cord
winding through fingers, a staircase
for angels, the lightfeet of anything
returning to wings.

Morning

All these years not knowing what it was
I was praying for. Storm, lightning-stroked
sky, the illumined

inside of things. How close rain
veined down the window is an entire cloud
ravelled in your palm. Now everything

slipping from brilliance. Your face each morning
blinking back the light, the small-fist way
breath challenges the clarity of glass

and loses.

∿∿∿

There are degrees of waking, small statics
of eyelash, cilium, the bow-fine
strings of light, arms taut

with reaching. There are the crownings,
chin lifted from chest
            that first

unfolding sun, the whole-note way
you circle me,   edgeless —

and the loss
behind it, the whole
ache & sigh
          wane

∿∿∿

pram-ride wobbly, sky
another chrome handle
distortion   tubular,

                    slipping

          through fingers, straws
                    of light, your outstretched   hand

∼∼∼

every circle of skin now, every
wing-rooted breath, fumbling, delicate

this bell-of-tulip readiness
this just-over-the-trees pink

eyelid flight, zygote fuschia
the budding fingertip

answers you will never question:
the open-map way of her palm, the receiving

          light

CIRCLES, CONCENTRIC

Spinning plates, that's what this is, rubbing my belly
and patting my head at the same time. I can't

think about it. The small swellings of the body, budding
limbs. While I separate the darks from the lights

your first tiny muscle contracting, first dip of wrist,
whorl of the ear. Finger rays sprouting forth, pigment

of the eye. This could be the moment
your heart separates

into its four chambers, when blood channels
its way back, that first

moment of return.

REASONS TO BELIEVE IN

"Now that we have seen each other," said the Unicorn, "if you'll
believe in me, I'll believe in you. Is that a bargain?"
"Yes, if you like" said Alice.
                                        — Lewis Carroll, *Through the Looking Glass*

Aperture.

What you might have seen from the inside:
star fissure, radius, tadpole sway

of the cellular, circular, fish-eye ancient
light. The fine gravity

of floating. Drift and root. Telaesthetic
clarity, a current

light-hearted, singing. The winnow
of orifice, its thin waters divining

aureola, the slit light windows
of the heart.

Light,

light that will return to you
in star and wing-beat, epithelial

sky, the vertebra to vertebra stringed
bone light of stepping

stone, passage. The *itsy bitsy*
fingertip-up-the-spine

pia mater, tender mother
unfurlings.

Unicorns.

Rabbit-hole darkness, its routes
of gradual sky.   A lure

of spired cloud, any light that draws you
pacing,   a voice

a voice through water, spindled aster
far, far, away the wheeling

happily, all those possible
hooved endings

Surfacing.

little-hilled
island of the heart, baby-fisted
sponge of salt, salient

not like the stone's baldness
but the ripple
when it sinks, the ever-expansive

arc of reaching, how the heart might look
if it had arms, palmate, like the inside-out hunger
of a starfish, whole,   beaming —

Silence.

alveoli, polyp
the many-flowered
density of breath

air has never felt
so littered, words
such decay

Stairways.

every moment of lifting, the finger to finger
breadth of shoulder, the 6 lb, 7 ounce weight

of bewilderment, that which I could never imagine
holding, but do, somehow, as I tense up the stairs, each rise

a breath, each breath a foot-along-floorboard
hesitation, a chance of ground

to carry us

First Bath

even water isn't pure enough
    to take away the first   *(salt of us*

shiver   when toes curling
    you are dipped   *little fin, wet feather*

when inner-arm empty from across
the room   *wing-tucked, shell-curved*
a nurse's hands unfold

my abdomen, purple-gilled, membraneous,

and just moments before, the cave-touching
of the just-gone-blind, of the fused
angles we know without light:
        elbowswrist anklesknees shoulderneck
           ear, splay
           of hand

and here are the unboned, the eyes
underwater violet, the iodine
inside heatlamp, iris
bulbous, the fully dilated
night

              forgive me

this harsh hush-a-bye light, the splatsplat of blood
on tile, the spaghetti arm strength for two oranges, water,
for the small contained bodies of the familiar, but not

for this, forgive me
the beads
sapid gold &
fishegg delicate, the only light I had for days
drawn in eyedroppers, black
nipples, the weary

expression of every drop

that will fall
and miss
your tongue

Variations on a Blue Sky
for Grandma R.

dandelion seed, iris-flecked,   drifting

sun slumped in a twist of cloud,   your daughter's body
                                          holding you
                         like a bed you slept in
                            once, soundly
                                          the wrist
laid to land, the wrist

                               fuelled in copper, pressed
                    to the whorled listening
                       of the thumb

pale-faced, paper plate
                    white, scallop-edged,   balancing

                    cupcake froth, the sun
                    a first birthday candle,   *your wish*
                                          snuffed in cloud

party-hat conical, circus-tent
vaulted, the eye
inward-vented, open,   the eye
turned on itself,

                    or the freshcut green of Uncle G's soles
                    tinted head-over-lawnmower, the dog-ear
                    twitch of storm, annelid tremolo
                    in grass, the spasmodic way he stopped
                    seeing,

9-1-1 vibrato   the space between
                                     voice
                    and hearing, body-silent, full of wind. A flag

on the other side of glass,   rippling. A fluid-armed circling,

>   mouth miming
>   *mother   mother*

shades of tea with milk, shades of dust
swept from corners,   sun,
>   a pillaged gold, a penny
>   shrouded in the palm
the heat

>   a child's fingers, pining
>   room to room,   the bleat of white
>   sheepbody, knitted
>   spines of cloud,   a hinged air

>   that reminds you
>   there is no hiding
>   from wings —

SNOW ANGEL

If this is the end, let it be, little dove,
a string in the wind like sand

from a palm, a pigeon's leg strung
to a woodblock, snagged by barbed wire.

Let it be the *Y* of your wing shadow
open-jawed above coyote's trail, feathers locked

in a stark questioning of sky. Or another glass-
stunned winter, the hole in the snow

where I interrupted
your death, my hands

shocked in the weight
of that which was made

for carrying — Let it be
the smallboned sparrow-

curve of the palm, any vestige
of homing, that depression

in snow where your heat had already
glossed over, where the twirled skirt

of a flailing wing could have been any
message, lifting.

REFINEMENT OF THE HAND

What Makes Sense To the Hand

Might be weight, the uncalculated
lift of chickadee from finger, the swerve
of your shoulder or a response
to water, opening —

might be the small habits
of touch, a stranger's hand becoming familiar
in music or time, the curve
of a girl's face streaked in dust. Might be

instinct, animal against
skin, turning apples from peel, pages
from knowing. Might be the dark,
wet feathers between thighs, the soft
forming of bone, dip

of fontanel. Might be bloom,
water shifting in a bucket, compensation
of shoulder, memory of spine.

Might be cards, dealing
chance and luck, holding some things
close to the heart

or loss, the clutching
of small histories: seed packets, a nail file,
clipped pictures of your mother, the prick
of a stray pin.

BERRY PICKING

It's all about pathways, blood,
the calyx-lit compass

of wander. Patch to patch
this is refinement of the hand, a family

clustered every August in the plinkity-plink slow
task of gathering. It's all about love

measured in buckets, pies, the familiar round dance
of birdsong, season. Or small returns,

wild raspberry
straight to the tongue,

grandma's yip-yip yodel
through trees, your straw hat

drifting the *swee-swee-sweet*
meadowlark dusk.

✺

This is the way, you say, to grandma's deep-dish pies,
the latest invention swinging in your hand, five rusted nails
in a wooden paw. This is

the way to the abandoned
wrecks of metal, old Indian camps, car-frame skeletal,
entire plants raked out by the roots, the loot
of our sticky-fingered greed. This is the way to her hands,

grandpa, cocoon-pale, the fine-grained
flit of ghost, birch bark, palms
cast in the glowing chalk
of the moon,   this is the way

to plenty, small pauses
between trees, the hunched shadows of her footprints
in moss, silent-   flexing.

Not Confession

This is not to confess, but to apologize for that car ride
after berry-picking, the day I tipped a full bucket over
my stubborn head, purple-thumbed locked grandpa's keys in
he trunk, swigged back the last of the orange crush
in the backseat vinyl stick '76 Olds, berries jiggling
my teeth, fingers stained sweet, your peach scarf on my head
like a sunset, *Grandma, grandma grandma I want to swim! jump!*
splash so big my waves will tip a whole
family of loons.

That day in the middle of my own lake, the only day you ever
tossed words over me, a sudden current of berries, blue
ripe-skinned tears.

HEARTY

This is not about dexterity
but showmanship, the old bear in you
scavenging about the dump, raising your dukes
to a cub who cleaned out two candy wrappers in one lick,
oblivious. This is you

grandpa, with the yellow lenses so big they light
the corners of your mouth, caution-sign-
in-headlights brilliant. This is you
after quadruple by-pass surgery holding out
your plate for the fat

and gristle. And these are your hands, grandpa,
fingers thick as rungs lifting me
to the black x's in your chest, a cheater's game
of tic-tac-toe or crisscrossed at the chicken-wire gate

any excuse to enter
the garden. This is you straightening the stakes
with grandma's old pantyhose, folding back
the leaves, a shirt collar,
as if this was the first time you have looked
for signs of ripeness, something whole to return
                                    to seed

a tomato in each palm
sunwarm,   dusty

DROWNING IN AIR

I always told you they could
feel it. Even in death
they never stop looking. Just like you
in that watery coffin, your one red eye
winking.

Beneath our boat, a mobile
of lines, lullaby of lures.
We fish for pride, for streamers
of wire smiles to drag behind, to keep alive
selectively in buckets, the gaping
gills and that one lidless eye

burning in light. You were scared to death
of drowning, never wore a life jacket, but here you float
forever in my mind, that last breath burst
across your face, giggle of water
in an overflowing tub, the throaty sputterings
when grandma opened the drain. Imagine

the slowest possible drowning,
water exchanged for air, sip by sip, fish. Imagine a silver
chain in grandpa's hands, beads slipping
between fingers, a last prayer
and a man so thin he whirligigs
down the drain.

The joke is that you drowned in air,
your own breath, and that's all
breath is, a thinness
separating you from death: a tin
boat, claw-foot tub, a hollow
rusted lung.

ICE FISHING

You are not saved
by winter's crust.

We reel you in carefully, fractured
scales of light through ice
your body a scar
of constellations.

You are cold, the way my feet are often cold,
straight through bone. One eye in snow, one
to the sky. Your last breath
an orange-blooded rust,
melting snow.

Muscle thick with current, death
is long, a relentless tail-smack
back to the hole.

Sun-swollen ice puddles. A widening
eye. Pupils grow rainbow-lashed
parhelions. Throat-tempo
behind closed eyes, walls and walls
the smell of fish.

Fillet-sizzle, flesh spits back.
A wet blot on the gutting block
fading. Your face
between scales, plates
of broken mirror.

MOTH LAKE, FISHING ALBUM
for Great-Grandpa D.

Dusk
  Bass in your hands is a limp lung sighing, gills loosen
  lichen strands, thin pellucid mouth.

  Hook dropped only a foot
  and I know you can't see how far my line goes
  below the surface. Disappointment is your rod bending
  a tight line, torn spine.

Rescue
  Pickerel on the dock (not breathing but eyes alive, scales
  and scales of green sky) Grandpa at the gutting block, my
  foot curving fish belly, white on white, cool mushroom-
  skinned fish slipped to the edge of
  the edge, gills —

Dragged by the mouth
  a fighting muscle
  how do you know it doesn't hurt?
  hook-ripped lip
  how can you know scales torn from cheeks, or hook
  piercing mouth and eye?

What the gills sing
  fish death is what the eyes eclipse, what the body, *the softness*
  of a sleeping hand, what the gills, *a hand inside music*, what
  the mouth, *shredded tongues*, what the scales *filled with sky,*
  filled with sky

  and when you slip from my hand what piece of lake
  on the dock left, what hole in the water
  what drifting

in your hand, fish stomach and tired waves
beautiful mouth, slack agape sky
beautiful fin, a feather

pike hung at the gill cleft, clear lake fins and
your hands the same limpid ghosts, eyes
the dark center of blood, scent of tin

pointing to a loon family, your palm draws
dusk, water-smooth neck, a throat call —
for a moment you have forgotten

jack snagged with green jelly lure and beside you
a pale girl prays through teeth for all the fish to
swim, to swim —

BLUEBERRY PIE (FROM THE UNWRITTEN RECIPES)

Blueberry pie begins in the forest with buckets and patience.

Pastry

spin & score, spin & score
a giant petal, flour-white, dimpled
berry drum rolling
one by one, tones
of indigo to azure
whole-note spoonfuls
of rolling skies

Filling

berry pulp loosens
seed, a lake
of love notes, waterbeetles
scribble-dancing
all afternoon, the smallfeet
tango of bee
and pistil, the lengthening
sun, stemmed thirst
of sepal

Timing (one song, danced)

this is where you begin: in the vinyl drip
of a syrup-slow air, the slack dust-

twirl of storms echoed
in the roots of your hair,
backlit

over   & over,
the needle bleeds Billie, *Long Gone*
hips reel his hand to your weight-
less,   water languid
limbs, arms sway
the timing of waves

purple finger-
tips, lips
syncopated

kisses, random
perfections of a pebble-
ellipsed shore

PICOT

How you pulled loops of coloured thread
through canvas and grew
this vase of flowers,

how your hands found stillness
in the rhythm of petit point
the push, loop and pull

music held there, in thread shadow.

How it took five shades of green
to sew the light of a leaf

(and for each thread
pulled from your palm, a deeper
crease —   I will touch

your handwriting, feel warmth on my shoulders, press
perfume behind glass, frame
five generations of light.

How I will look for stillness
in the stitches flowing, a direction
of waves pointing
          to some beginning
                    or end.

HIGHWAY RECITATIONS (YOU LEARN GOING HOME)

The reason for the sky is the Earth,
for the Earth the sky.
                    — Anne Szumigalski

i.

the distance:
wing-trimmed sky
        falling behind
        in grey
                    clippings

distal rain —
veins
        and veins

back of hand spitting blue

this land, a wrist bone
pulsing sky

ii.

Vista Nursing Home

I am seeing you seeing
me awkward, pale-
skinned and hungry when you ask:
when am I going home?

iii.

highway recitations:
Grandpa's deer whistles streaming sky,
all the way home a shrill cry

sing it:
iiiiiiiiiiiiiiiiiiiiiiiiiiiiiiiiiiiiiiiiiiiiiiiiiiiiiii

iv.

trying to hold on to myself because it's all I've got to show you

v.

small talk
driving past the flood along sky-bruised land
is this what Kerouac meant when he said he could see
through the earth?

vi.

power lines losing ground,
river rising, swollen fields,
a chain of crucifixions

vii.

what you miss the most is wings
thrumming at the feeder
we talk holding hands, humming
in your bones, birds
willing flight

viii.

tulips
ripe yellow,
petals spouting rain

       — what you saw the last time you lived April

now only acrid air,
flowers choking you

like the candy you swallowed
when you heard his body, fall
water-heavy, fail   *take those flowers away*

ix.

if only we could see the entire road from here:

x.

wings of morning light, branch-hatched
sky, when you close your eyes
what is the first colour?

xi.

fill your palms with sky-belly, watch
your knuckles course the land

IN AND OUT OF LIGHT

BLUE

Preserves
the whiteness in things, the intermediate,
between grass and sky, a ghost
twilight tints beneath skin, the nobility
of blood.   A flicker
inside woad leaf, blue
is a stain
the eye drifts to, tails
of smoke, anything fleeting.

SNOW, A SMALL SPRING

Flags of sun, icicles filled
with light, mercury rising. Somewhere

a home. Ageless

snow, you lie
as if just fallen, but it's been
a whole season of waiting.

∼∼∼∼

The old light draws us
closer each morning. Eyes remember
a time of waking. Something about
a dark room

opens us, loosens,

leaves and time
   falling

∼∼∼∼

even the wind is aging now, even the grains
ice-shifted and skittered, tumble
stone over breaking
stone

∼∼∼∼

Spoon-grey sky chimes
mouthfuls of cloud. Music takes longer
to fall in this
air before rain. Trying

to let my entire head rest
in your hands, can't remember
how to release the neck
completely, even in sleep we hold onto

∼∼∼

these places
even in death
one last time
before learning.

∼∼∼

Snow dust in sun, diamond air.
The sparrow, long-lashed
eye of the willow
watches
at its window, you,
a shadow in a blank
white room. Snow pretends

∼∼∼

the city is clean,
sweeps the eye from the last
efforts of the dead. Leaves

lost in rain's opaque
afterthought, a light that purls you

back every morning, the horizon
torn in your wake.

what are the last words to be when the field, muddy, fills with rain, when the mouth puddled in its own tongue fumbles, when the marigolds wait in deep blue tubs and the hens and chickens fatten, when cream cups, butter drops, milkweed scatter, when dill umbels ripe-yellow, seed themselves, when I stop promising to return

PERCEPTION AT A DISTANCE (NOTES ON LEAVING)

i. recital, arterial

The room is too small for this
there is no room

for dying. You have been here before,
the backward light
march to the window, the sun breaking you

one last time. Your daughter's hands
out of reach   posed ivories   at the key

      hovering

ii.

You learn to leave like you learn an instrument
or mothering, slowly, in scales, *one arm, two, head through*

the hole day by day, repetitive. The half-written
notes to yourself, the thread-on-the-thumb failings:

ember element glow, fingerprint swirls
where there used to be

memory.

iii.

Dream begins in water, breath,
the two incompatible ways we learn

to love. Home is any dark
sip of tea, any water

approaching the boil, this pressured
air, everything telling you

to stop —
the back, the brain, the strings pulling down the corners

of your mouth. The metronome wag
of the tongue. The curtains you want to draw

when the sun cuts through, the frayed-
edged light.

iv.

Windows now, withdrawal
insidious as glass, the panes
and panes, between us, your refracted
eye. Or the glasshouse memory. So clear
and removed. All those little jelly jars
where there used to be plenty. A sun
falling through, a polished light.

v.

If I knock now, will you hear me?

Garden shadow. The between weeds umbra
crusted earth. *Hello in there.* Bean seeds shriveled
in their faded paper. Lanterns burnt, swaying.

And the spider plant
as old as me, its babies
dropped, for years
without rooting, for years
its whiskered dust.

A Reason To Reach

Who are we to talk weather when you haven't felt
the sky on your face for days *weeks*, when the sun only
lights your hair when you sleep and the hours *so many
hours* are all the same endless
       & ending

Storm. Rise and fall of dust, locusts.
Tell me again about that summer
when the sky lowered a giant blue wing
and standing in a field with the air so wide you found
a reason to reach.

Speak to me what your hands knead, what thirst
for a blueberry pie seeps, warm in the ribs, syrup-soaked
crust, what our teeth, pine-shadow blue
flash, when you turn from us
what hunger.

This Room, Rhythmic

Questions I want to ask but don't
for fear the answers will empty you.

How the silence when we leave reaches
the window, breath-bloomed mimes
the cloud of your sleep, a pressured sky.

How the mouth empties itself, jaw-gaped,
shadowed from a lifetime of words that no longer
work. You breathe the room rhythmic and we
draw closer, listening as we would to waves
or flame, for a moment becoming a slower breath
of ourselves, and you —

everything about you lightens, but the eyes
are sinking, moss-crept stone, and in this distance
you don't need to look, to be seen or found
for *the eyes*, you would tell us, *are for the waking*.

In and Out of Light

My fossil, my salt-faced doll, Grandmother
your eyes are deep as salt nests
in the depressions of stone, and the days are piling
helplessly like waves.

<center>~~~</center>

Goodbye and bloodless hands, lips
dough-cool, the loose of my mouth

empty. In the warmth of you, learning my own
cold fingers. And it doesn't matter
what I say, or don't, what
news. At the end
of your bed, my fingers small
in afghan loops, lost.

And where am I now? the room
a silence of questions
unanswered.

<center>~~~</center>

Sleep enters often, you roll
in and out of light, insistent
sun tires you.

Look! Look! Look! You refuse to see
the subtle changes, believe every day is the same
window, the same white
wren nest growing the same
egg of snow. Wings beating the same stone-
cold wind, cloud-
shorn sky.

And for a moment I believe you.

∽∽∽

Pearl strand above my chin, lifted
a smile. It's hard and simple to reach you. Hard
because I say the wrong things and simple
because time has left us. The body, an hour we live

over and over, the curtains close, we dream
backwards, lighten

skin and bone, water and air. We fall
and rise a stream over stone.

∽∽∽

The hand loosens, without task, without
words, the space between us widens
a slack jaw.
                    Goodbye, twice
        goodbye,

we might never have to leave.

        (sometimes the answer comes
        before the question)

If we had another day —

SPRING

This emergence of the dead — an iridescent
rainbow parting from wings, the undecided
eyes of the half-closed
or open — it's stepping around

loss, refusing to see
the patterns earth makes when the dead
dissolve: feathers, scattered
seed, what grows in spite of
our resistance.

CROCUSES, AN APOLOGY

Had it been any other year
I would have written, pressed silver
petals from luminescent fields,
would have sent you
a bucket of rain. Had it been

any other spring I might have asked
about drought, the divination
of sky, metal fishing boats and cracked
mirrors, about seven years
of dying, or luck
and all those nights of drowning.

Had it been any other day
the crocuses might have bloomed
like never before and spring's swift
breath, evanescent blue, might have welled
across these dead, dry fields.

～～～

Winged seed. Little larkspur blue. Haze and haze.
Pulsatilla, pulsatilla. Can you feel it? That first silken
cleave of rain.

～～～

Spray-painted carnations. I didn't want another
flower to dry, the silent apology of each
broken leaf, another poem
in the throat, crumpled, or that fake
colour that would never fade, your face

painted as if it were alive, as if it could feel
goodbye leaning over it, the poem's last
air, a fine paper
folded and folded

∾∾∾

I wanted to send you down diamanté, with as much light
        as the earth
could bear, down down with the hummingbird, rubythroated
air, a hover of dusk
on your eyelids, cross-stitched routes
to spring, grandpa's kerchiefs
knotted in trees, every turn
of sky that has prepared you, every light
however small, the paths
from garden to gate to door

DIAMOND

1.

When it was something I wished for
with eyes closed in cotton-candy light, a music box dancer
unwinding like a band of gold
twirled 'round the finger, when there was comfort in small
resistances, a penny in the palm, a button done,
undone, when light stroked the walls
like a mirror ball and you were a girl in rollerskates
going to the chapel, when you were waiting to be rescued
just like Penny and her diamond-hearted bear.

2.

How you twirled it like a prayer, silent-counting
each small point of stone in the thumb,
each claw. Sixty years of flesh
grown around, the raised callous
of rolling pin, wet cotton, a rhythm
you wring out each night
in your bones. How faithful this imprint
even in death, the gold slipping
like a key, right back into place.

3.

And now the honeycomb walls
sun-buzzed, twirling
the tutu-tufted sequin

uplight of your granddaughter's face, *her brilliant*
face elixir of wonder, so far from mine,
anything that sharp, that
broken

4.

What I want to believe in is precision, the cut
of your last breath, a tilt of the hand
to the window, a diamond
so filled with sun it shears the walls a confetti
of uncharted stars, in a light that escapes
just as it begins, unnoticed —

If You Could See Me Now

on the other side
of a ghost
watching steam gauze
the air above my cup
counting clouds
like all those little storms
that never broke.

If you could see me
trying to write
the ring they cut
from your swollen finger, if you knew
that when I held your hand I felt
the part of me that is dying, and if only
you could have seen, just yesterday
your scarf tied under my chin, the moment
I realized what you meant
when you spoke of
the ache in the wind.

On How I Might Preserve You

The way a rose bowl magnifies
bloom, pigment suspended like a dance
in a velvet skirt, if I could capture
your breath in glass and hold
to my ear your voice over water, if above
your lip a petal
fluttered and we could learn how to breathe
in the dark in our underwater
dreams, if the glass didn't cloud like a pill
in water, if breath didn't shatter
like light inside those diamond droplets
reeling
down the window.

A History of Blood

"So who will come tell us the depth of these ocean abysses?"
— Sri Ramakrishna, *The Salt Doll Parable*

SALT DOLL

"Who are you?" said the salt doll to the sea. The sea smilingly
replied "come in and see."

— Anthony deMello, *The Song of the Bird*

wrapped,

prayer inside
prayer, the cone of my hands
palm to palm, rag-clouds

of moon   tombed
salt, the eye's full
sail, white white open

a child's hands
delivered in a wave, a lustre

effloresce effloresce

~~~

finger-shrined, this yellow glow
of bone you pray for,
this leaving, every breath a crystal
held from the tongue, every wave
your predicted
ending,   how lustral

the strings of shoreline would be, the cheek to cheek
descent

if you were to fall
the watery watery
                    heart

~~~

were you not meant for hands, any term
of containment, the surface measure of a wave
apart from its reaching?

is this not about blood,
but portholes, the thin-pane
threat of rain, my girlhands

wanting to save
every drop
that would reel you?

～～～

heart behind glass, reliquary
any smallbird caged, stirring

a totem of palms,
hand above
hand,   the heart
passed,   the salt
        of every spilt
        hour, every wave   *Now I know*
                                    what I am

                turning

A History of Blood

I have looked for a rhythm, a thread
passing through one heartbeat
and out another, a motion
weaving pages, stories
binding stories

— the journey of my blood.

Birth dates, death dates,
a hyphen resting in-between
(a drawn eyelid), a crease
in history

(The salt doll is 100 years of tears
evaporated, preserver of secrets.
            She travels with blood,
mother to daughter gathering
ages, prayers, flower petals
            press them gently —

Turning pages, I was sifting soil
not for the sake of earth
but to find some treasure hidden
in those black lines, pressed
onto paper, letters
bent into words, whispering
a face, a name

She is the taste of oceans crossed,
            breath that carries.
She holds the rising steam of tea and sweat,
            childbirth on her skin.

The history of blood reveals in halves:
half-breed, half-blood, half-truth, I was left
with only half story
the unnamed, unspoken:
A Cree Woman

She is nine generations steeped
into one small apparition, distilled
mothersalt, the sharp edge of brine.)

∿∿∿

Margaret Matilda Hourie

Affidavit of a mother signed in script:

"I, Margaret Matilda Hourie, am a half-breed, head of a family"

   blood rushes

∿∿∿

Ravelled strands,
your name so neatly
executed. The hook of each
letter, little broken handles, a cup
in the earth, shards. White-

pixeled, the page is taking over, the page
is bleeding x's, *sign here* intersections, points
of inevitable crossings.

∿∿∿

Drawing history from veins,
I am learning the equation
of mixed blood, the face

of my salt doll: infinite grains
pouring . . .

I hold her lightly
for fear she'll lose her shape, spill white
between my fingers.

~~~

Tongue tip to her face — taste
the salt and dust of tears

silence   shifting

SALTATIONS

1. Inheritances
Where rain has eroded her: pores.
The skin of my salt doll, an ivory paste,
flour stirred with sea.

Berry lips, rasped and cracked,
her braids, feather-plaits
vaned in flight, *(the chained*
weight of the hand

2. Listening with palms
This line, a skin we share.

Grandmother, I wear you
a crease, thumb to wrist.

Everything I have seen
pleated in my palm, the rim of your skirt, a lifeline,
full as a bell.

Where we have grown: silver thread,
stretching

3. Her taste
Forehead sweat
in rain. Watch her dissolve
grain   by grain

shoulders   neck   eyes

opaque and
tracing heartlines

Shape lost
like the peal of your name in my mouth
before I learned you

Flora   *Flora*   *Flora-*

Bell

Country Wife

Isaac Batt, willing to be as great a brute as his Indian companions, absolutely forced one of his wives, who had recently lost her infant, to suckle a young Bear.

—— Samuel Hearne

StoneMaidenCreeMaidenIndianMaidenMother

Bloodlock. Wedlock. Out of
everything, duty.

An oblong of stone, moss-swaddled
grave, sunken chimney, an eagle's ghost-
path of smoke. Sorrow

circles here, the thin-wristed
rings of aspen, trembling areola
tough as bark, sapping. Night

is dirt
over dirt, fistfuls
of piling stars, the flickering vernix
of your body *your tiny body* dusted

in earth. Shards of creamware,
bone. A tinkling cone
at my hip, pupa wind
of your hair.

On all fours
the sweet dead-
fall earth.

~~~

Hunting me down like a hive, breasts
all swarm and sweet
needle-claw stinging.

Here is the hunger of blindness,
the numb refuge of the womb
when the animal draws in, in,
that hot colostrum balm.

~~~

in situ

little curled roots
of the ear, alula feather, bone

does what is left have anything to do
with what is found, the charcoal horizon
where her eyes never saw light, a humus
wet with womb

does what is left have anything to do
with flint, the small depressions
to the East, kaolin pipebowls, honey-coloured
chert,

just tell me
does it have marrow
ferruginous root
evidence of burning?

NESTICHIO

A child was born and at the age of 6 was stolen by the Indians.
When A. Spence came to the country several years afterwards, he
saw this white child among the Indians. He adopted her and later,
at the age of 12, took her for his wife.

— family archives

i.

I am daughter of your father's son of father son
of father. Six-years-old, salt-skinned and in feathers
when I am found and rescued, found
and fathered, found and stolen and lost and
married, 12-years-old who stole
who?

ii.

My mother, my bear, I am waiting
in the milk lit night, in the seven stars
of your hair, one for each
child lost, I am
dizzy with bees, maw
of sweet ash, heavy
in the back, stumbling.

iii.

They say you are dead, but either way
these hills grieve you, they wander
like a thin-lipped waft
from his pipebowl, like a blood
not meant to be shed, or sons
fallen in the thick braid of pine,
in the silent exchange of breath
for burning.

iv.

I can feel it in the leaves, 200 years
of decay, in the excavated clasp
knife and its dull, folded light. I can
feel it in the white-
tailed corners of the eye, in the pine
all twisted up, the shadows of mane and rope-
wrapped hands.

In flint, the steadiness of bone, mother,
beneath big game trails and that old-ankled
bark, I can feel it, buckling
in the littered humps
of chimney, the land
a sloughed smoke, heaving
your unsettled grave.

BONE LIGHTENING

GRAVEYARDS

You pace stone now, the way you paced boxcars
on the graveyard shift, alone, looking for
the nearest exit.

Hands that never come clean. A house
of evidence, fingerprints
on everything you touch. Time served
and blood thick as oil. If I could lay

a penny on the track for each
lost night of sleep, every Christmas morning
o/t shift, I might buy back
your soul. Early on I learned

vanity, how to lie
to protect you, told my friends
that's my dad in the engine while the truth
slept with arms crossed
in the switchback of dawn, in the blood-shot
caboose walls, between-car flashes
of sky.

Now thirty-three years
of leaving that one long night
carved in your face, that start
and end you counted on. The grief

that reminds you of permanence. The crook in your back
as you bow into the day, the scar-glare steel
of tracks studded in your mind over and over
the bells the bells that have buried your fathers

here where you stand
strong as a forehead, bald
as stone.

Ride of the Skeleton

This is the chorus of your labour, china rattle against the glass
of my sleep, dreams of dirt swept from a caboose floor,
the scrub of daybreak hauling garbage bags, paper towels,
toilet soap, coffee mugs, CN perks that pile in our home
like a derailment.

To find the drawings you left, bones etched in boxcars,
sunglasses and silhouettes, motorcycles in purple sunsets,
to read the lyrics scratched in oil-stained ties, the bone rattle
dance of a teenage father, to hear the train like you did,
from the inside, a long drum roll —

Freight train shivers in the weight of steel, files car by car through
a narrowing horizon.

PASSENGER

Something about the train and its rat-rat-rattling, the tattling
wing of engine light, a giant moth catching night's ghost
limbs, trees half-spun in frost, the breath-gauzed window
of a man open-mouthed, cocooned in a blanket, drooling.

Things we are privy to in the half-light will be left
unsaid in the morning: auroral faces of a stranger's
dream at the window, the open-vault creak of boxcars, sinking
metal, the steel passage of a rail moon etching the night silver.

BEFORE

The first thing I will notice when we meet —
blue night thickening your hair and eyelids
rimmed pink, the beginnings of sunrise.

The first thing I will do is squeeze your hand and feel
a pattern in your bones
cold with age I don't yet know, but recognize

somehow —
I will forget this silence, this before
and after we are together, when you are here
and I am learning once again
how to be your daughter.

APPLES
for O.

What fruit is our store,
what flower?
— H. D.

The apple because it is deeper than blood
and straight into its light you look
without forgiveness. Because my hands trembled

all day like the boiling pots of crabs, pulp
in jelly bags wavering atop their fine fleshed

threads. And when he climbs out
onto a limb and shakes, I laugh
at how ungraceful this is, fruit split

on concrete, the little buggers rolling off
in all directions. Because the blooming
beginnings of rot was the best

we could do, sweet brown buckets
of fingerprints, small bruises of greed.

Because the apple is a mouth
waiting to be opened, a vowel
I'm still waiting to learn, a word

just one, I want to grow
between us, a forbidden
blush of skin, the slit-in-the-skirt
map of thigh, arrows.

Because he tried to help
and got it all wrong, saved the pulp
instead of the juice and sent the whole thing
whirling down the drain.

Because his forearms, little root systems
of earth and cedar press sweat, the sweet
wet apple air.

Because May-apple, wild
lemon, fire-lobed leaves,
and your open-palmed readiness.

Because you teach me how to taste, directly
from the fingers, the long-lick dip and scoop ways
you might empty me.

Because spring in the grove is awkward-limbed, beautiful
and the zen flower blooms with the whole season behind it,

and tonight the sky, a fruit we thirst for, a blizzard

of petals, unruliness, the flesh-round requests
of desire. And because the apple tells time

by ripeness, surrender, and all we know,
all we know is resistance.

BEAR

I promised never to return, but I do, I wait
like a lover waits, somewhere between fear
and hope, for the weight of black
across white shell sand, the tramp
of your heart to crack shore. I wait

inside water, the bone lightening
river, that quick
lick of sand, erasure
or a chance

to be saved, for the body to forgive
like water, make me believe
we were never here. I cannot say

for certain if it was me
or the river that cried, if it was current or bones
that lay down between stones
and died or if I am already forgetting

fear, how it is only one letter away from
your shoulders, the black eruptions of earth
stripped from shadow, how the waiting is
so much longer in the dark.

HUNGER

Hunger is what the dog becomes, hung
from the clothesline, paws floating
the ground a novice marionette. It's auditioning
for death, that narrow exit, a lonely cameo
of a stray sock fading.

Hunger is close by, next door, a girl
jig-sawed by a chicken-wire fence
watching the dog watching a door
that never opens.

Hunger is aquarium, life behind
glass, trusting that which has never
touched you. Hunger is the hollow spaces,

dipping in
and out, the ripple
of a swallow in puddles, the cat
with the bird whose one good wing beats
beneath a heavy paw.

Hunger is everywhere: sun through glass
through leaves, immeasurable scales of light, a pause
before an answer.

Hunger is a book unread,
its tender creamy flesh
and black pepper pores.

Hunger is night, blindness,
a hand on the wall, a switch
out of reach, desire
and no room for questions.

Hunger is without maps, a child's drawing
in black, Josefov museum and charcoal
permanence, eighty-thousand names
etched in stone, frozen
veins of marble.

Hunger is life
slipping between your legs, a burning
ring at the pit of something
that scares you, a small mouth
dark and rooting.

THIS FRACTAL HEART

INSCRIPTION

A woman I know is waiting
comma-curled at the hips
for the rest of her
sentence. Her body
outlined in body is a girl
on the cover of a book
reading from a book
with the same cover. Fractal,

her heart a page
where the words
start over, where the blood,
each fine-brushed
stroke, *closer closer*, arrives
a new entry.

DELIVERY

This is the narrow palsy
of the heart, raw pulse
of passage. *Yeah yeah as if you really believed in*
The roundness of it. *My mother*
rubs my back, she knows, *she*
knows how close
to dying this is. How very close
to heat. The beginning is. There are no corners
in this room. No turning back, no
To be thy name, oh!
my mother
Give us this
surrender
This is what they tell you, *for thine is the*
to hold this in, to father
small mouths, kingdoms
The power and the glory
forget. *Amen.*
Regret. *Deliver me from*
How very close —

FIRST NOTES

Could it be
this simple,

the heart
pure and brief

as a note,

that moment of emptiness
before song, a string of whole notes
rising from wire, the chorus of wings?

Or the iris pierced open
in raw light, the wide-thaw
nimbus of spring. A departure

just the same as the arrival:

water   entering
water

the infinite

r i n g s

~~~

Pupil's fluidity. The horizon bowing down
to what has come before: your death-
shocked eyes, those two small notes
dilating, a reason to believe

this is not your last light.

~~~

Flit

& lift. Wingtip catches sun. We share

this big dream sea. Starfish. Angel. Lilt-of-wing
heart. The impossible

ease. There is only room for
this: resistance
and the efficiency of wings.

༄༄༄

My hand for the first time
on your back, the foxtail tickle
of the palm, dandelion shine
on the wrist where the sun, jaundice,
flicks and flicks.

༄༄༄

Milk needles down, weeps
for those small open spaces
we name *home*, the root of that
first note, mouth around
areola, that long and milky *o* —

CLAY BONES

Fine china doll, white schist. You cast
bones soft as clay fishes, slip me
a red silt skin.

Breech birth is spired
ankles, pigeon knees,
finger rays reaching
for the underwater bell
of your heart.

You press palms into spoons, pinch
a small key of clavicle, seal fontanel
with a bowl
of whispers.

NIGHT BATHS

> She wanted to swim far out, where no woman had swum before.
> —Kate Chopin, *The Awakening*

It is this that scares me: your body
crossing ocean, the steady pull
and drift of waves, reckless shorelines
and the way you might have been thrown
like a baby out with the bathwater.

It is this air when you return, the lingering
but subtle salt, the way you learned
weightlessness, how to walk alone into water
without longing.

Or how much I remain the daughter
who doesn't want you to swim
where no woman has gone before,
who wants you here
at my girlbed, in the *goodnight sleeptight*
drift of your silhouette at the door, in a bell

of bathwater rising, the porcelain
chime of dream, in the deepswirled heart
held to each ear, the long-whirled
tugging of the drain.

MIRROR

Now and again the mirror holds me
like water, shows me the shape
of forgiveness, the cradled egg-curve
hollows of the arm, the static-float
hair shimmer of my left hip, where it rises
into waist, waits
for hand, the open breath
of disclosure.

What the mirror kept from you, the other-side-
of-the-room window, any indication
of light, celation of the eye
veering. How many times
it undressed you, probed your skin
with its flat glare, floated you
down its stagnant water, drowned you
belly-up in shame.

(SMILE)

The silence around
your mouth, laugh lines
I will inherit, the whispered language
of parenthesis, an inside cue
to smile (now) pose the appropriate
question (a drink?) the precise
pressure a cold cloth relieves
from his (drunken) head, the mists
of perfume it takes to conceal (a lover's)
desire, the perfect temperature
to burn the breakfast (ever-so)
slightly, when to leave
a faint smoke
on the tongue.

WATER DAMAGE

It's all water under the Berber carpet now, but that sopping
musty underlay still haunts me. Sour, lacking-air water,
finding-its-way-to-the-lowest-places-then-sitting-there water.
It was just a small crack in our foundation, but the damage *oh*
the damage.

And it wasn't the water really, but the stagnation, the mold.
What grew without our attention. That small, insistent life.

And that warm salty gush so distinctly clean, so like my own
flesh while I stood at the counter slicing a cucumber, that sharp
citrus dripping down my thigh, how it rolled from the top
without direction, found its way
out. For a moment wanting
to wipe it away, but you wouldn't let me, love, no
on the glass those first breaks
toward breath, spiny microscopic

unfurlings. Now with each rain we are reminded
of our imperfections, those neglected spaces that pool
and stare back, what water will not
forgive: cracked tile, silent weeping.

CLOTHESLINE

Lulled to sleep in the light hiss
of sun-sipped snow, puddles of widening
sky, river's thorny ice. It is this,
grass and the brittle tips of the dead that give me
hope. Dog dotted in burrs, wind-combed
fields, the opening
of water, resurrection. I don't want you
to see behind us, our shadows stretched,
what depends too much
on light, the forgotten
clothes on the line, faded
and wavering.

Grief of the sun in its longing, high shadow cutting-through-wind kind of arrogance. We walk behind a stroller, biting wind, the smell of old leaves drawn up in the wheel. I am thinking of forgiveness and if it's worth it, remembering how the sun draws a crack in your face, forehead of bark. There are some things that will never get through. This

mirror of river that peels us away from stillness, this idea of one direction. You point to the stick lodged in the bank, how it fights, its polished skin. We are good at this, not leaving. But you understand me, why I refuse to retrace my steps, why I turn my back to the bridge behind us, its drawn bow pointing, its one raised eyebrow.

Transplant

1/

We have pulled our roots and now we are dead-
drifting leaves trying to settle into this
frozen ground. Suddenly the bed
is back porch empty. Everything so clean.
I want dust. Something to rely on. Something

to avoid. That last walk through, the imprint
of room in the body, grain of wood, that old stretch
of yourself. How it doesn't seem possible
to leave, that hole in the ground clutching,
that blue velvet purse, frozen

the last time we breathed
one body. This earth
the spring will inhale
carpel, placenta, the severed
umbilical routings.

2/

How do you transplant an angel?

When the ground shifts, sucks up
growth and pokes you in the belly
with baby finger roots.

When you are loose, a little empty in the pouch
and her hands jiggle you in the bath, all plump
and pinch.

When the quill tip bleeds
a ripe pulp of rain

and where the feather
scabs snow, all winter
the halo, where the crow flags
the moon.

3/

Everything you don't come with: a history, instructions
how to grow one. You can't

blame a home, you tell me, it grows
from you, your willingness
to begin again.

FALL, ONE LAST LETTER

Another season preparing
to fall without you. I can't believe
you are not seeing this. This change
of light in the fields, the golden thread of summer
pulling away.

Branches open sky, the babe
in my arms, her language of new
skin, *lanugo,* a wispy white. In the letter
I would write *she's beautiful,*
grandma, angelic. Would you believe

I watch the birds now, finally
have the patience for it. I'm beginning to
understand how the wren spoke to you
in a way we never could.

The streets are a hiss of crumpled letters,
the seething unaddressed. I roll the pram
through loss, float beneath
streetlamps, spokes flickering
like the nascent beginning
of wings. The honesty

of her face scares me. Makes me want to give
too much. Feel the limitations of
love. It's raining

leaves and each leaf a letter
I forgot to write. Sky, a negative
of earth. Branch, a positive
of root. If I could just give you

this: one last look at light, her
star-cut eye, the precision
of ear, a paper heart
folded in two, or the sky
when she reaches up
her first touch of cloud, that
kind of wholeness.

POETRY
for my parents

That I still can't say the word to you,
book maybe, *homework* even
but not *poetry*, something so frivolous,
unnecessary, so without limbs.

Sometimes I can't say it to myself
when I come home and her mouth is all sticky
with fruit, eyes wild
with new language. A world without me.

How can I say this to the abandoned
beach of her memory, the fall wind of her shoulders
always a bit defensive, leaning away. Or my own fingers on keys
tap-tapping into a room, a window
half-naked, dressed in leaves.

What if I told you it never made sense, the apology
of hotdog carts on a Friday afternoon, the briefcase black
Portage Avenue and the vendors hunched, the littered
head-down haul of it.

Or the empty beach trails, all that washed up
glass. How can I show you that even waste
can be beautiful, that even brokenness can end —

The Lewis Carroll quote in "Reasons to Believe In" is from "The Lion and the Unicorn" in *Through the Looking Glass* (Wisconsin: Whitman, 1955).

The epigraph for "Blueberry Pie (from the unwritten recipes)" is from an imagined conversation with my great-grandmother.

In "Highway Recitations (you learn going home)", the Anne Szumigalski quote is taken from her poem "Goodbye" as it appears in *Voice* (Regina: Coteau Books, 1995).

The introductory quotation to the section "A History of Blood" is excerpted from an apologue by Hindu mystic Sri Ramakrishna as reproduced in Pierre Laszlo's *Salt: Grain of Life* (Columbia: Columbia University, 2001).

The Anthony De Mello quote in "Salt Doll" is from "The Salt Doll" in *The Song of the Bird* (New York: Doubleday, 1984).

The holograph in "A History of Blood" is a reproduction of my 4th generation great-grandmother's signature as it appears on a Métis scrip application from April 7, 1850 (courtesy of the Manitoba Métis Federation through Public Archives Canada).

The salt doll in "Saltations" is an inheritance I received from my great-great grandmother Flora Bell Tapper.

The epigraph to "Country Wife" is a reference to my 9th generation great-grandfather, Isaac Batt as noted in Samuel Hearne's *A Journey from Prince of Wales's Fort in Hudson's Bay to the Northern Ocean* (Toronto: Macmillan, 1958).

The epigraph for "Apples" is excerpted from H.D.'s "XXVI" in *The Walls Do Not Fall* (London: Oxford University, 1944).

"Velvet purse" in "Transplant" was termed by Liz Philips.

ACKNOWLEDGEMENTS

Thank you to the editors of Prairie Fire, Event, Descant, The Fiddlehead, tart, NewWest Review, Spring, CV2, Qwerty, portfolio milieu 2004, and Other Voices for publishing earlier versions of some of these poems and to CBC radio for broadcasting the birthing poems.

I am grateful to the Saskatchewan Arts Board for support that contributed significantly to the early developments and final editing of this work and to the Sage Hill Writing Experience and Saskatchewan Writers Guild for community.

Thank you to my mentor extraordinaire, Sylvia Legris, for being the first to suggest the absurd — that I might actually be working on a book. Also to Liz Philips, Steven Ross Smith, Tim Lilburn, Hilary Clark, Dave Margoshes, Erin Mouré and Mariianne Mays for every gesture of encouragement.

Wings to Erin Bidlake for the early readings and to Miranda Traub for being such a genuine example of faith.

Feathers to Julia, Lisa, and Sylvia for Abbysitting and to Olivia and Felix for Thursday mornings.

Leaps and curtseys to my editor-with-wings, Seàn Virgo, for introductions to the pillow sprites and the most generous offerings of ear and heart.

Always, thanks to my parents for taking such good care of family. And finally, to Darren and Abby for being everything that makes this possible — home.